Collins

Cambridge IGCSE™

Chemistry

WORKBOOK

Chris Sunley

William Collins' dream of knowledge for all began with the publication of his first book in 1819.
A self-educated mill worker, he not only enriched millions of lives, but also founded a flourishing publishing house.
Today, staying true to this spirit, Collins books are packed with inspiration, innovation and practical expertise.
They place you at the centre of a world of possibility and give you exactly what you need to explore it.

Collins. Freedom to teach.

Published by Collins
An imprint of HarperCollins*Publishers*
The News Building, 1 London Bridge Street, London, SE1 9GF, UK

HarperCollins*Publishers*
Macken House, 39/40 Mayor Street Upper, Dublin 1, D01 C9W8, Ireland

Browse the complete Collins catalogue at
collins.co.uk

10 9 8 7 6 5 4 3 2 1

ISBN 978-0-00-867086-3

Acknowledgements
With thanks to the following teachers for reviewing materials and providing valuable feedback: **Gauri Tendulkar**, JBCN International School; **Dr Rahul Sharma**, IRA Global School; and with thanks to the following teachers who provided feedback during the development stages: **Shalini Reddy**, Manthan International School, **Sejal Vasarkar**, SVKM JV Parekh International School.

British Library Cataloguing-in-Publication Data
A catalogue record for this publication is available from the British Library.

Author: **Chris Sunley**
Expert reviewer: **Gauri Tendulkar**
Publisher: **Elaine Higgleton**
Product manager: **Jennifer Hall**
Copyeditor: **Clodagh Burke**
Proofreader: **Aidan Gill**
Cover designer: **Gordon MacGilp**
Cover artwork: **Drawlab19/Shutterstock**
Internal designer and illustrator: **PDQ Media**
Typesetter: **PDQ Media**
Production controllers: **Sarah Hovell and Lyndsey Rogers**
Printed in India by Multivista Global Pvt. Ltd.

MIX
Paper | Supporting responsible forestry
FSC™ C007454
www.fsc.org

This book is produced from independently certified FSC™ paper to ensure responsible forest management. For more information visit: www.harpercollins.co.uk/green

Cambridge International Education material in this publication is reproduced under licence and remains the intellectual property of Cambridge University Press & Assessment.

This text has not been through the endorsement process for the Cambridge Pathway. Any references or materials related to answers, grades, papers or examinations are based on the opinion of the author(s). The Cambridge International Education syllabus or curriculum framework associated assessment guidance material and specimen papers should always be referred to for definitive guidance.

The publishers gratefully acknowledge the permission granted to reproduce the copyright material in this book. Every effort has been made to trace copyright holders and to obtain their permission for the use of copyright material. The publishers will gladly receive any information enabling them to rectify any error or omission at the first opportunity.

Photographs
p 34 Shutterstock/Peter Sobolev, p 40 Shutterstock/Ajamal

Contents

Contents

Answers for all the questions in this Workbook are available from
http://www.collins.co.uk/internationalresources.

Solids, liquids and gases

Student's Book pages 10–15 | Syllabus learning objectives 1.1.1–1.1.4;
SUPPLEMENT 1.1.5–1.1.6

....

1 How are the arrangement and movement of particles in a solid different from those in a gas?

....

.... [2]

2 How do the arrangement and movement of particles in a liquid differ from those in a solid?

....

.... [2]

3 What apparatus would you use to measure the volume of a liquid?

.... [1]

4 Look at the particle diagrams below.

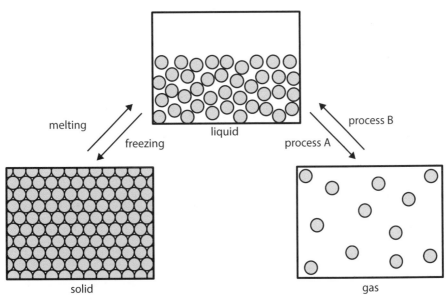

Label the two processes marked on the diagram.

Process A: .... [1]

Process B: .... [1]

5 Look at the diagrams below.

A   B

a What change in temperature would make balloon A look more like balloon B?

.... [1]

b What change in pressure would make balloon B look more like balloon A?

.... [1]

TIP
Check your understanding of the kinetic particle theory in the Student's Book.

6
SUPPLEMENT
Use kinetic particle theory to explain the changes that occur when a solid turns into a liquid.

....

.... [2]

7
SUPPLEMENT
Use kinetic particle theory to explain the following:

a The effects of increasing pressure on the volume of a gas.

....

.... [2]

b The effects of reducing temperature on the volume of a gas. [2]

....

....

Diffusion

Student's Book pages 16–18 | Syllabus learning objectives 1.2.1; SUPPLEMENT 1.2.2

....

1 A perfumed candle is lit to provide a pleasant smell in a room. Use the kinetic particle theory to explain how the perfume spreads through the whole room.

....

.... [1]

2 A spoonful of sugar is added to a cup of tea with a temperature of 30 °C and another spoonful of sugar is added to a cup of tea with a temperature of 60 °C. Use the kinetic particle theory to explain the differences in the rates of diffusion in the two drinks.

....

.... [2]

3 SUPPLEMENT Use the idea of relative molecular mass to explain why nitrogen gas will diffuse more rapidly than oxygen gas.

....

.... [2]

TIP

Remember: nitrogen and oxygen are diatomic.

4   The following table shows the relative molecular masses of some common hydrocarbon gases.

SUPPLEMENT

Hydrocarbon	Relative molecular mass
Methane	16
Propane	44
Butane	58

Which of these hydrocarbon gases will diffuse at the slowest rate when mixed in a room full of air? Explain your answer.

....

.... [2]

Elements, compounds and mixtures

Student's Book pages 24–25 | Syllabus learning objective 2.1.1

> **TIP**
> The Periodic Table only includes elements.

1 What is the difference between an element and a compound?

....

.... [2]

2 What is the difference between a compound and a mixture?

....

.... [2]

3 Complete the following table by selecting the correct description.

Substance	Element	Compound	Mixture
Sea water			
Sodium chloride			
Copper(II) sulfate solution			
Iron			
Diamond			
Distilled/pure water			

Substance	Element	Compound	Mixture
Oxygen			
Carbon dioxide			
Air			

[9]

4 Look at the diagram below. Each of the spheres represents an element.

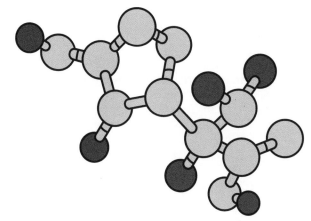

a Does the diagram represent an element, a compound or a mixture?

.... [1]

b Explain your answer.

....

.... [2]

Atomic structure and the Periodic Table

Student's Book pages 25–27 and 30–33 | Syllabus learning objectives 2.2.1–2.2.6

1 State whether the following statements are **True** or **False**.

Statement	True or False
Protons are found in the nucleus	
In an atom, the numbers of protons and neutrons are always the same	
Electrons are arranged in shells around the nucleus	
An electron has a relative mass of 1	
A proton has a relative charge of +1	
The nucleon number gives the number of protons and neutrons in the nucleus	
An element with an atomic number of 11 has three electron shells	

[7]

TIP

When answering questions about atomic structure, make sure to have a copy of the Periodic Table to hand (included on page 124 of this Workbook).

2 Complete the following table.

Atom	Atomic number	Nucleon number	Number of neutrons	Number of electrons	Electron arrangement
$^{7}_{3}Li$					
$^{19}_{9}F$					
$^{28}_{14}Si$					
$^{31}_{15}P$					
$^{39}_{19}K$					

[5]

3 Look at the Periodic Table on page 124 and then answer questions **a–e**.

a Which Group is nitrogen in?

.... [1]

b Which Group is calcium in?

.... [1]

c Sodium is in the third Period. How many electron shells does it have?

.... [1]

d Oxygen is in Group VI. How many electrons does it have in its outer electron shell?

.... [1]

e What do the final electron shells of all the noble gases have in common?

.... [1]

4 The drawing below shows an atom diagram.

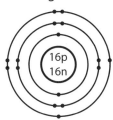

Taking information from the Periodic Table on page 124, draw atom diagrams of the following elements:

a Aluminium [2]

b Magnesium [2]

c Neon [2]

Isotopes

Student's Book pages 27–30 | Syllabus learning objectives 2.3.1–2.3.2;
SUPPLEMENT 2.3.3–2.3.4

TIP
You need to be familiar with these terms: proton number/ atomic number and mass number/nucleon number.

1 Look at the atomic structures of these two atoms:

$$^{63}_{29}\text{Cu and } ^{65}_{29}\text{Cu}$$

a How do you know these atoms are isotopes?

.... [1]

b State **one** feature of the atoms that these isotopes have in common.

.... [1]

2 Chlorine has two common isotopes: $^{35}_{17}Cl$ and $^{37}_{17}Cl$.

SUPPLEMENT

Explain why these isotopes of chlorine have the same chemical properties.

....

.... [2]

3 Use the data in the following table to calculate the relative atomic mass of magnesium.
SUPPLEMENT Give your answer to 3 significant figures.

Nucleon number	Relative abundance (%)
24	79
25	10
26	11

....

....

....

.... [2]

Ions and ionic bonds

Student's Book pages 38–44 | Syllabus learning objectives 2.4.1–2.4.4;
SUPPLEMENT 2.4.5–2.4.7

....

1 Chlorine forms the chloride ion Cl^-.

a Has the chlorine atom lost or gained an electron?

.... [1]

b Why is only one electron lost or gained?

....

.... [1]

c Is the chloride ion an anion or a cation?

.... [1]

2 Sodium chloride is a solid at room temperature.

a What holds the solid structure together?

.... [1]

b Why does solid sodium chloride not conduct an electric current?

.... [1]

c Would you expect sodium chloride to have a high or low melting point? Explain your answer.

....

....

.... [2]

3 ▶ Use the atomic numbers in the Periodic Table on page 124 to help you complete the table below.

Element	Electron arrangement of the atom	Electron arrangement of the ion	Charge on the ion
Sodium			
Fluorine			
Potassium			

[9]

4 ▶ Draw dot-and-cross diagrams to show the formation of the ionic bonds between the following elements. In each case, write the formulae of the ions formed.

TIP
You will need to use the atomic numbers of the elements as shown in the Periodic Table on page 124.

a Potassium fluoride

[2]

b Lithium chloride

[2]

5 The following diagram represents the structure of lithium chloride.

⬤ chloride ion ◯ lithium ion

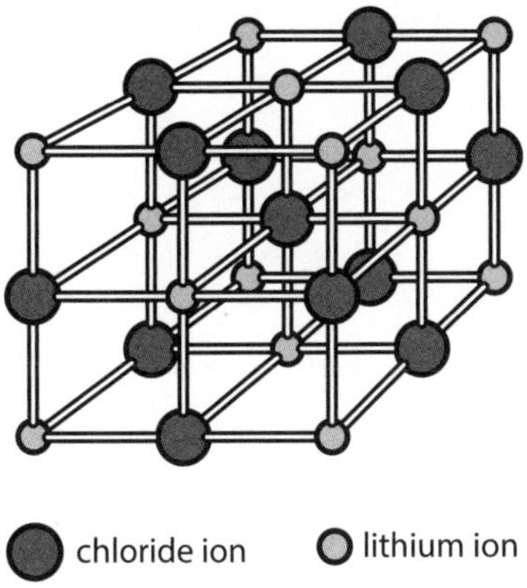

a What does the diagram show about the structure of lithium chloride?

....

....

.... [3]

b Explain why lithium chloride conducts electricity when molten or in solution.

....

.... [2]

c Explain why lithium chloride has a high melting point.

....

.... [2]

Draw dot-and-cross diagrams to show the ionic bonding in the following compounds. In each case, write the formulae of the ions formed.

> **TIP**
>
> Use the same approach as in Chapter 2 of the Student's Book.

a Calcium oxide (proton numbers Ca = 20; O = 8)

[2]

b Aluminium chloride (proton numbers Al = 13; Cl = 17)

[2]

Simple molecules and covalent bonds

Student's Book pages 47–52 | Syllabus learning objectives 2.5.1–2.5.3;
SUPPLEMENT 2.5.4–2.5.5

··

TIP

For dot-and-cross diagrams, use the same approach as in Chapter 2 of the Student's Book.

1 Use a dot-and-cross diagram to show how the covalent bond is formed in fluorine, F_2. The proton number of fluorine is 9.

[2]

2

a Use a dot-and-cross diagram to show the covalent bonds in phosphine, PH_3. The proton number of hydrogen is 1 and the proton number of phosphorus is 15.

[2]

b Will phosphine conduct electricity? Give a reason for your answer.

....

.... [2]

c Would you expect phosphine to have a low or high boiling point? Give a reason for your answer.

....

.... [2]

3

SUPPLEMENT

a Draw a dot-and-cross diagram to show the electron configuration of propene, C_3H_6. The proton number of hydrogen is 1 and the proton number of carbon is 6.

[3]

b Explain, in terms of structure and bonding, the reasons for this simple molecule having a low melting point and poor electrical conductivity.

....

....

.... [2]

Giant covalent structures

Student's Book pages 52–55 | Syllabus learning objectives 2.6.1– 2.6.2;
SUPPLEMENT 2.6.3–2.6.4

1 Use the diagram showing the structure of graphite to answer the questions below.

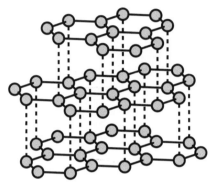

Structure of graphite

a What do the complete lines in each layer represent?

.... [1]

b What do the broken lines between the layers represent?

.... [1]

c Explain why graphite can be used as a lubricant.

.... [1]

2 What property of diamond makes it useful as a cutting tool?

....

.... [2]

3 Use the diagram showing the structure of silicon(IV) oxide to answer the questions below.

SUPPLEMENT

a Would you expect silicon(IV) oxide to have a low or high melting point? Explain your answer.

....

....

.... [3]

b Would you expect silicon(IV) oxide to act as an electrode in the same way that graphite does? Explain your answer.

....

....

.... [3]

SUPPLEMENT

Metallic bonding

Student's Book pages 58–60 | Syllabus learning objectives SUPPLEMENT
2.7.1–2.7.2

1 The diagram below represents the structure of a metal.

 SUPPLEMENT

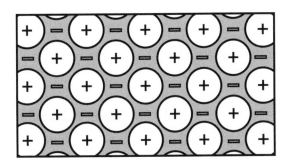

TIP
Check you know the meaning of 'delocalised' – refer to Chapter 2 in the Student's Book.

a What are represented by the circles with + signs inside?

.... [1]

b What are represented by the – signs?

.... [1]

c Use the diagram to explain why metals have good electrical conductivity.

....

.... [2]

2 This question is about the properties of metals.

SUPPLEMENT

a Metals are ductile. Explain what this means.

.... [1]

b Metals are malleable. Explain what this means.

.... [1]

3 Look at the information in the following table.

SUPPLEMENT

Substance	Melting point (°C)	Electrical conductivity	
		When solid	When molten
A	3550	Poor	Poor
B	660	Good	Good
C	801	Poor	Good

a Which of the substances is a metal?

.... [1]

b Explain the reasons for your choice.

....

.... [2]

Formulae

Student's Book pages 66–75 | Syllabus learning objectives 3.1.1–3.1.4;
SUPPLEMENT 3.1.5– 3.1.8

....

1 Deduce the formulae of the following compounds:

TIP
Use the Periodic Table to on page 124 identify the combining powers of the elements in the compound.

a Sodium oxide

.... [1]

b Hydrogen sulfide

.... [1]

c Aluminium chloride

.... [1]

2 Deduce the chemical formulae of the following compounds:

a Copper(II) sulfate

.... [1]

b Calcium carbonate

.... [1]

c Sodium hydroxide

.... [1]

3 Look at the diagrammatic representation of ethanol. Deduce the formula of ethanol.

$$H-\underset{\underset{H}{|}}{\overset{\overset{H}{|}}{C}} - \underset{\underset{H}{|}}{\overset{\overset{H}{|}}{C}} - OH$$

.... [1]

4 Magnesium burns in oxygen to form a white powder which is magnesium oxide.

a Write a word equation for the reaction, including state symbols.

.... [2]

b Write a balanced symbol equation for the reaction, including state symbols.

.... [2]

5 Methane burns in oxygen to form carbon dioxide and water.

SUPPLEMENT

a Write a word equation for the reaction, including state symbols.

.... [2]

b Write a symbol equation for the reaction, including state symbols.

....

.... [2]

6 Write down the empirical formula for each of the following compounds:

SUPPLEMENT

a Ethene, C_2H_4

.... [1]

b Hydrogen peroxide, H_2O_2

.... [1]

c Butane, C_4H_{10}

.... [1]

TIP
Refer to the Student's Book on how to write ionic equations.

7 Copper(II) ions react in solution with hydroxide ions to form a precipitate of copper(II) hydroxide. Write an ionic equation, including state symbols, for this reaction.

SUPPLEMENT

.... [3]

TIP
In an ionic equation. remember that the charges on the positive and negative ions must balance/cancel each other out.

8 Balance the following equations:

SUPPLEMENT

a ___$Cu(NO_3)_2(s) \rightarrow$ ___ $CuO(s) +$ ___ $NO_2(g) +$ ___ $O_2(g)$ [1]

b ___$CaCO_3(s) +$ ___$HCl(aq) \rightarrow$ ___$CaCl_2(aq) +$ ___$CO_2(g) +$ ___$H_2O(l)$ [1]

c ___$Fe^{3+}(aq) +$ ___$OH^-(aq) \rightarrow$ ___$Fe(OH)_3(s)$ [1]

d ___$H^+(aq) +$ ___ $CO_3^{2-}(aq) \rightarrow$ ___$H_2O(l) +$ ___$CO_2(g)$ [1]

Relative masses of atoms and molecules

Student's Book pages 76–81 | Syllabus learning objectives 3.2.1–3.2.3

1 Calculate the relative molecular masses of the following compounds:

a Water, H_2O (A_r: H = 1, O = 16)

.... [1]

b Propane, C_3H_8 (A_r: H = 1, C = 12)

.... [1]

c Nitrogen dioxide, NO_2 (A_r: N = 14, O = 16)

.... [1]

d Phosphorus pentachloride, PCl_5 (A_r: P = 31, Cl = 35.5)

.... [1]

2 Explain why the relative atomic mass of chlorine (A_r of 35.5) is not a whole number.

....

.... [2]

3 Calculate the relative formula masses of the following ionic compounds.

a Sodium chloride (A_r: Na = 23, Cl = 35.5)

.... [1]

b Calcium carbonate (A_r: C = 12, O = 16, Ca = 40)

.... [1]

c Aluminium hydroxide (A_r: H = 1, O = 16, Al = 27)

.... [1]

4 Use the equation and the relative masses given to calculate the answers to **a–c**.

TIP
Start with the atomic or molecular masses of the chemicals mentioned in the question. You will then need to scale up or scale down the quantities using the same scaling factors for each element/compound.

a $C(s) + O_2(g) \rightarrow CO_2(g)$ (A_r: C = 12, O = 16)

6 g of carbon is burnt in excess oxygen until the reaction is complete. What mass of carbon dioxide will be formed?

....

....

.... [2]

b $CuO(s) + H_2(g) \rightarrow Cu(s) + H_2O(l)$ (A_r: H = 1, O = 16, Cu = 64)

Hydrogen is passed over heated copper(II) oxide in a combustion tube. 10 g of copper(II) oxide is used. What mass of copper will be formed?

....

....

.... [2]

c $CaCO_3(s) \rightarrow CaO(s) + CO_2(g)$ (A_r: C = 12, O = 16, Ca = 40)

Calcium carbonate is heated until the reaction is complete. 4 g of carbon dioxide is produced. Calculate the mass of calcium carbonate used. Give your answer to 2 significant figures.

....

....

....   [2]

The mole and the Avogadro constant

Student's Book pages 81–92 | Syllabus learning objectives 3.3.1; SUPPLEMENT 3.3.2–3.3.8

1 ▶ 20 g of sodium hydroxide (NaOH) is fully dissolved in 500 ml of water. Select the correct concentration from options **A–D**.

(A_r: H = 1, O = 16, Na = 23)

A $20\ g/dm^3$

B $1\ mol/dm^3$

C $0.5\ mol/dm^3$

D $2\ mol/dm^3$

....   [1]

TIP
Remember: $1000\ cm^3$ is equivalent to $1\ dm^3$.

2 A student has been asked to make a solution of calcium hydroxide with a concentration of 0.1 mol/dm^3. Select the correct combination from options **A–D**.

$$(A_r: H = 1, O = 16, Ca = 40)$$

A 74 g of calcium hydroxide and 1000 cm^3 of water.

B 74 g of calcium hydroxide in 250 cm^3 of water.

C 7.4 g of calcium hydroxide in 1 dm^3 of water.

D 3.7 g of calcium hydroxide in 0.25 dm^3 of water.

.... [1]

3 A student has been asked to make 100 cm^3 of a 0.1 M solution of hydrochloric acid starting with 1 dm^3 of a solution of hydrochloric acid with a concentration of 0.5 mol/dm^3. Select the correct combination from options **A–D**.

A 10 ml of 0.5 M and 90 cm^3 of distilled water.

B 20 ml of 0.5 M hydrochloric acid and 80 cm^3 of distilled water.

C 40 ml of 0.5 M hydrochloric acid and 60 cm^3 of distilled water.

D 50 ml of 0.5 M hydrochloric acid and 50 cm^3 of distilled water.

.... [1]

4 Which of the following statements about the Avogadro constant is correct?

PPLEMENT

A 1 mole of sodium chloride contains 6.02×10^{23} molecules.

B 1 mole of carbon dioxide contains 6.02×10^{23} ions.

C 0.5 mole of carbon contains 3.01×10^{23} atoms.

D 12 g of carbon contain 1.204×10^{24} atoms.

.... [1]

5 Calculate how many moles are in the following.

SUPPLEMENT

a 4.6 g of sodium (A_r: Na = 23)

....

.... [1]

b 32 g of methane, CH_4 (A_r: H = 1, C = 12)

....

.... [1]

c 7.8 g of aluminium hydroxide, $Al(OH)_3$ (A_r: H = 1, O = 16, Al = 27)

....

.... [1]

d 45 g of glucose, $C_6H_{12}O_6$ (A_r: H = 1, C = 12, O = 16)

....

.... [1]

6 The following apparatus can be used to calculate the volume of carbon dioxide produced in the reaction between calcium carbonate and dilute hydrochloric acid.

SUPPLEMENT

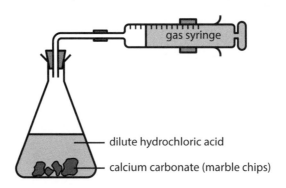

gas syringe

dilute hydrochloric acid

calcium carbonate (marble chips)

The equation for the reaction is:

$CaCO_3(s) + 2HCl(aq) \rightarrow CaCl_2(aq) + CO_2(g) + H_2O(l)$

An experiment was performed using the following two quantities. Use this information to answer the questions.

0.4 g calcium carbonate

50 cm^3 of 1 M hydrochloric acid.

a   How many moles of calcium carbonate were used? (A_r: C = 12, O = 16, Ca = 40)

....

.... [1]

b   How many moles of hydrochloric acid were used?

....

.... [1]

c   Which of the reactants was in excess?

....

.... [1]

d   Calculate how many moles of carbon dioxide would be formed when the reaction was complete.

....

....

.... [1]

e   Calculate what volume the carbon dioxide would occupy at room temperature and pressure. Give your answer to 3 significant figures.

TIP
Remember: the molar gas volume = 24 dm³ at r.t.p.

....

....

....   [2]

7

A sample of magnesium was heated until red hot in a crucible as shown in the diagram below:

The lid was then lifted slightly to let oxygen in but prevent the loss of magnesium oxide.

a   Write a fully balanced equation for the reaction between magnesium and oxygen to form magnesium oxide.

....   [1]

b   In the experiment, a 100% yield was achieved and 4 g of magnesium oxide was produced.

   i   Calculate the mass of magnesium used (A_r: Mg = 24).

....

....   [2]

ii   Calculate the volume of oxygen used (molar gas volume = 24 dm^3 at r.t.p.).

....

.... [2]

iii   If only an 80% yield had been achieved in the experiment using the quantities calculated in parts **i** and **ii**, what mass of magnesium oxide would have been produced?

....

.... [2]

TIP
An empirical formula shows the simplest whole number ratio of the atoms in a compound.

8 **SUPPLEMENT**   Butane has an empirical formula of C_2H_5. Its relative molecular mass is 58. Calculate the molecular formula of butane.

$$(A_r: H = 1, C = 12)$$

....

.... [1]

9 **SUPPLEMENT**   Silicon dioxide (SiO_2) is extracted from the ground and purified. What is the percentage composition by mass of silicon and oxygen in silicon dioxide? Give your answers to 2 significant figures. ($A_r: O = 16, Si = 28$)

....

....

.... [2]

Electrolysis

Student's Book pages 108–119 | Syllabus learning objectives 4.1.1–4.1.7;
SUPPLEMENT 4.1.8–4.1.11

....

1 Use this diagram of some electrolysis apparatus to answer the questions that follow.

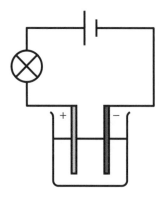

a What name is given to the two shaded rods in the diagram?

.... [1]

b What inert materials can be used for these rods?

.... [1]

c What name is given to the rod marked with a plus sign?

.... [1]

d What name is given to the rod marked with a minus sign?

.... [1]

e The bulb in the circuit lights up. What name is given to the type of liquid in the beaker?

.... [1]

2 Using the same apparatus as shown in Question 1, an electric current is passed through molten sodium chloride.

a What product will be formed at the rod marked with a plus sign?

.... [1]

b What product will be formed at the rod marked with a minus sign?

.... [1]

c If the substance in the beaker is solid sodium chloride, explain why no electrolysis will take place.

....

.... [2]

3 What products are formed in the electrolysis of concentrated aqueous sodium chloride solution?

a At the anode:

.... [1]

b At the cathode:

.... [1]

4 What products will be formed in the electrolysis of the following molten compounds?

a Zinc oxide.

i At the anode:

.... [1]

ii At the cathode:

.... [1]

b Silver bromide.

i At the anode:

.... [1]

ii At the cathode:

.... [1]

5 A student has been asked to design an apparatus to electroplate an iron nail using a silver rod.

a Sketch the apparatus that the student could use for this electroplating. You should show:

i the electrical circuit

ii the positioning of the silver rod and the iron nail

iii a labelled electrolyte that could be used.

[3]

b Give **two** reasons why materials like iron might be electroplated.

....

.... [2]

TIP
At Supplementary level, explanations for the changes at the electrodes should include the ions involved and the products formed.

6 Molten magnesium oxide is electrolysed.

UPPLEMENT

a Explain what happens at the anode.

....

....

.... [2]

b Explain what happens at the cathode.

....

....

.... [2]

c Write an ionic half-equation for the change at the anode.

....

.... [2]

d Write an ionic half-equation for the change at the cathode.

....

.... [2]

e The changes at the anode and cathode involve the chemical processes of oxidation and reduction.

   i What is the change at the anode?

.... [1]

   ii What is the change at the cathode?

.... [1]

7

SUPPLEMENT

Complete the following table which summarises the changes that occur during the electrolysis of copper(II) sulfate solution using different electrodes.

Electrolyte	Electrodes	Change at the anode	Change at the cathode
Copper(II) sulfate	graphite		
Copper(II) sulfate	copper		

[4]

Hydrogen–oxygen fuel cells

Student's Book pages 119–121 | Syllabus learning objectives 4.2.1; SUPPLEMENT 4.2.2

1

a Write a word equation showing the chemical change in a hydrogen–oxygen fuel cell.

[1]

b Write a balanced symbol equation with state symbols for this reaction.

[2]

2 The following image shows a simple hydrogen fuel cell.

a The hydrogen gas is pumped into the positive electrode. What name is given to a positive electrode?

.... [1]

b The oxygen gas is pumped into the negative electrode. What name is given to a negative electrode?

.... [1]

c For the fuel cell to work, what must pass through the external circuit that connects the two electrodes?

.... [1]

3 Write half-equations for the following reactions in the fuel cell:

SUPPLEMENT

a Hydrogen gas forming hydrogen ions.

.... [2]

b Oxygen gas forming oxide ions.

.... [2]

4

SUPPLEMENT

a What are the advantages of using a hydrogen–oxygen fuel cell in a car instead of using petrol or diesel?

....

.... [2]

b How would you calculate the efficiency of a hydrogen–oxygen fuel cell?

....

....

.... [2]

c What are the disadvantages of using hydrogen–oxygen fuel cells in a car instead of petrol or diesel?

....

.... [2]

Exothermic and endothermic reactions

Student's Book pages 128–136 | Syllabus learning objectives 5.1.1–5.1.3;
SUPPLEMENT 5.1.4–5.1.8

....

1 Which of the following statements is correct?

    A An exothermic reaction absorbs energy from the surroundings.

    B An endothermic reaction releases thermal energy.

    C An exothermic reaction causes an increase in the temperature of the surroundings.

    D An endothermic reaction does not absorb or release thermal energy.

    .... [1]

2 Look at the diagram of the reaction pathway and then answer the questions that follow.

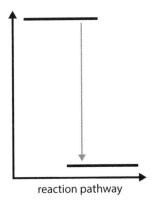

reaction pathway

a Label the vertical axis.

.... [1]

b Label each of the two horizontal lines linked by the downwards arrow.

.... [1]

c What type of reaction does this reaction pathway diagram illustrate?

.... [1]

3 The apparatus shown in the diagram was used by three groups of students (groups A, B and C) to compare the thermal energy produced by burning ethanol.

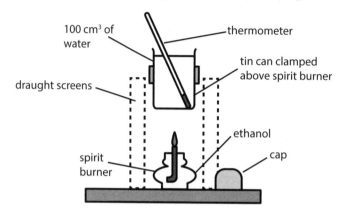

The results produced by the three groups (A–C) are shown in the table.

Group	Temperature rise of the water (°C)	Mass of spirit burner and ethanol before burning (g)	Mass of spirit burner and ethanol after burning (g)	Mass of ethanol burnt (g)	Temperature rise produced by burning 1 g of ethanol (°C/g)
A	34	52.2	51.4		
B	32	50.6	49.9		
C	36	51.4	50.5		

a Complete the second last column in the table. [3]

b Complete the final column in the table. Give your answers to 3 significant figures. [3]

c Which group's results show the highest thermal energy produced when burning ethanol?

.... [1]

TIP

Where you are asked to identify differences or errors, make sure you answer in terms of the actual experiment the question is referring to.

d Why was the water being heated in a tin can rather than a glass beaker?　　　[2]

....

....

e Suggest some reasons why the temperature rises per gram of ethanol were not the same for each group.

....

.... [2]

TIP
Where a question about a particular chemical term has 2 marks, you must try to give an answer that has at least two pieces of information.

4 Explain what is meant by the term activation energy, E_a.

SUPPLEMENT

....

.... [2]

5 A reaction takes place with an activation energy of 60 kJ/mol. The enthalpy change in the reaction is 100 kJ/mol.

SUPPLEMENT

a Draw and label a reaction pathway diagram for this reaction in the space below.

[4]

b State whether the reaction is exothermic or endothermic.

.... [1]

6 Methane (CH_4) burns in oxygen to form carbon dioxide and water.

SUPPLEMENT

a Write down a fully balanced equation for the reaction.

.... [2]

b In the first stage of the reaction which bonds must be broken?

.... [2]

c Is bond breaking an exothermic or endothermic process?

.... [1]

d The next stage of the reaction is bond making. Is this an exothermic or endothermic process?

.... [1]

e Methane is the main component of natural gas. Will the enthalpy change for the reaction, ΔH, be positive or negative?

.... [1]

7 Hydrogen burns in oxygen to form water.

SUPPLEMENT

a Write a fully balanced equation for this reaction.

.... [2]

b Calculate the enthalpy change for the reaction using the bond energy values given in kJ/mol. (O=O 498, H–H 436, H–O 464)

....

....

....

.... [4]

Physical and chemical changes; Rates of reaction

Student's Book pages 144–157 | Syllabus learning objectives: 6.1.1; 6.2.1–6.2.4; SUPPLEMENT 6.2.5–6.2.8

1 Which **one** of the following experiments involves a chemical change?

A Adding a spatula measure of sodium chloride to a beaker of distilled water.

B Mixing gas jars of carbon dioxide and oxygen.

C Putting a graphite rod into a beaker of warm water.

D Adding magnesium ribbon to a beaker of dilute hydrochloric acid.

[1]

2 State whether the following changes are physical or chemical.

a Boiling a kettle of water.

[1]

b Lighting a candle for a birthday cake.

[1]

c Using petrol as the fuel in a car.

[1]

d Adding sugar to a cup of coffee.

[1]

3 When copper(II) sulfate crystals are added to water in a conical flask, the water turns blue. Is this a physical or chemical change? Give a reason for your answer.

....

.... [2]

4 Magnesium ribbon reacts with dilute sulfuric acid producing magnesium sulfate solution and hydrogen gas. Describe an experiment that you could use to work out the effect of temperature on the rate of reaction. You have to use three different temperatures: 30 °C, 35 °C and 40 °C.

TIP
When measuring the rate of a reaction, you must be able to measure the time taken.

a In the space below, draw and label the apparatus you would use in this experiment.

[3]

b In the space below, draw a table suitable to record your results.

[3]

5 An experiment is used to compare the reactions of magnesium powder and magnesium ribbon with an excess amount of dilute hydrochloric acid.

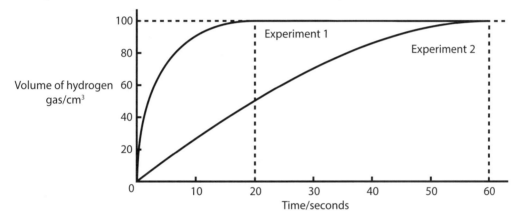

a In which experiment was the magnesium ribbon? Explain your reasoning.

....

....
[2]

b Why is the rate of producing hydrogen in Experiment 1 higher in the first 5 seconds than after 10 seconds?

....

....
[2]

c Why do both graphs level out?

....
[1]

d Suggest a reason why both graphs level out at 100 cm^3 of hydrogen.

.... [1]

6 Give **two** important characteristics of a catalyst.

1. .... [1]

2. .... [1]

7 **SUPPLEMENT** Using collision theory, describe and explain the effect on the rate of reaction of increasing the temperature in the reaction between marble chips and dilute hydrochloric acid.

....

....

.... [3]

8 **SUPPLEMENT** The following apparatus is used to measure the effect of temperature on the volume of gas produced when magnesium is added to dilute hydrochloric acid.

gas syringe

coil of magnesium ribbon trapped between bung and side of flask

dilute hydrochloric acid

a You have been asked to compare the rate of reaction at four different temperatures, using the apparatus four times. State **two** conditions that must not be changed in the four experiments.

....

.... [2]

b The magnesium ribbon will produce more than 100 cm^3 hydrogen, which is the maximum capacity of the gas syringe. What could you measure in the four experiments to see how the rate of reaction changes from one experiment to the next?

.... [1]

c Even when repeating the experiment four times very carefully, there are likely to be some experimental errors. List **two** ways that errors could occur.

....

.... [2]

9 State how a catalyst increases the rate of a reaction.

PPLEMENT

.... [1]

10 In the reaction between magnesium and hydrochloric acid, use collision theory to explain why increasing the concentration of the acid will increase the rate of reaction.

PPLEMENT

....

....

.... [3]

Reversible reactions and equilibrium

Student's Book pages 161–168 | Syllabus learning objectives 6.3.1–6.3.2;
SUPPLEMENT 6.3.3–6.3.11

1 Look at the following equation and then answer questions **a–d**.

$$CuSO_4.5H_2O(s) \rightleftharpoons CuSO_4(s) + 5H_2O(l)$$

a What name is given to compounds that contain water of crystallisation?

.... [1]

b What name is given to compounds that do not contain water of crystallisation?

.... [1]

c What colour change occurs when the copper(II) sulfate crystals are heated?

.... [2]

d After heating, how can the reaction be reversed?

.... [1]

2 When cobalt(II) chloride crystals ($CoCl_2.6H_2O$) are heated, the crystals turn to a powder and change colour. When water is added to the powder, the original colour returns.

a Write a balanced equation, with state symbols, for this reaction.

.... [3]

TIP
Remember to use the correct sign to show the change from reactants to products in a reversible reaction.

b What is the colour change when the cobalt(II) chloride crystals are heated?

.... [1]

c Suggest a simple laboratory test that cobalt(II) chloride can be used for.

.... [1]

3 State **two** features of a chemical reaction which reaches equilibrium.

SUPPLEMENT

.... [1]

.... [1]

TIP
Two industrial processes are important in this topic – the Haber process and the Contact process.

4 The equation below shows the industrial production of ammonia in the Haber process.

SUPPLEMENT

$$N_2(g) + 3H_2(g) \rightleftharpoons 2NH_3(g) \quad \text{Production of ammonia: } \Delta H = -\text{ve}$$

a Explain what $\Delta H = -\text{ve}$ means in this reaction.

.... [1]

b State the source of each of the reactants.

....

.... [2]

c Complete the following table (by adding a ✓) to show how the position of equilibrium is affected by the different conditions shown.   [4]

Change of condition	The equilibrium moves to the left	The equilibrium moves to the right	There is no change in the equilibrium
Increasing the temperature			
Increasing the pressure			
Removing the ammonia as it forms			
Adding a catalyst			

TIP

There are important links to the Rate of reaction topic.

5 A type of a reaction is shown below:

SUPPLEMENT

$$A(g) + B(g) \rightleftharpoons C(g) \text{ Production of C: } \Delta H = -ve$$

a A temperature of 700 °C is used. Explain why such a high temperature is used.

....

....   [2]

b A catalyst is used in this reaction. Explain why a catalyst is used.

....

....   [2]

6 In industry, sulfur dioxide is converted to sulfur trioxide in the Contact process.

JPPLEMENT

a Write a fully balanced equation for this reaction.

.... [2]

b List the conditions used in the manufacture.

i Temperature:

.... [1]

ii Pressure:

.... [1]

iii Catalyst:

.... [1]

Redox

Student's Book pages 172–177 | Syllabus learning objectives 6.4.1–6.4.5;
SUPPLEMENT 6.4.6–6.4.13

1 What is a redox reaction?

.... [1]

TIP
Make sure you know what oxidation numbers are.

2 What are the oxidation numbers of the metals in the following compounds?

a Potassium chloride, KCl

.... [1]

b Manganese oxide, MnO

.... [1]

c Aluminium oxide, Al_2O_3

.... [1]

3 In chromium chloride, chromium has an oxidation number of 3.

a Show how the oxidation number of chromium can be included when naming the compound.

.... [1]

b What is the formula of the chromium chloride?

.... [1]

4 Define the following in terms of oxygen:

a Oxidation

.... [1]

b Reduction

.... [1]

5   Complete the following table by adding a tick (✓) to show if each reaction is a redox reaction.

Reaction	Is this a redox reaction?
$MgCO_3(s) \rightarrow MgO(s) + CO_2(g)$	
$2Mg(s) + O_2(g) \rightarrow 2MgO(s)$	
$MgO(s) + H_2(g) \rightarrow Mg(s) + H_2O(l)$	

[3]

6   Look at the following equation and then answer questions **a**–**b**.

$$Zn(s) + CuO(s) \rightarrow ZnO(s) + Cu(s)$$

a   What has been oxidised in this reaction?

.... [1]

b   What has been reduced in this reaction?

.... [1]

7   Which of these definitions of oxidation is correct?

PPLEMENT

    A   A gain of electrons.

    B   A reaction which only involved oxygen gas.

    C   An increase in oxidation number.

    D   A reaction in which only oxides are formed.

.... [1]

8 ▶ Magnesium reacts with chlorine gas as shown in the following equation:

$$Mg(s) + Cl_2(g) \rightarrow MgCl_2(s)$$

a What is the oxidation state of magnesium in solid magnesium?

.... [1]

b What is the oxidation state of chlorine in chlorine gas?

.... [1]

c What is the oxidation state of the magnesium in magnesium chloride?

.... [1]

d What is the oxidation state of chlorine in magnesium chloride?

.... [1]

> **TIP**
>
> Check you are familiar with ionic equations.

9 ▶ Look at the following ionic equation and then answer questions a–b.

SUPPLEMENT

$$2Na(s) \rightarrow 2Na^+(s) + 2e^-$$

a Has the sodium been oxidised or reduced?

.... [1]

b What is the oxidation state of the sodium in the Na^+ ion?

.... [1]

10 Potassium manganate(VII), $KMnO_4$ is an oxidising agent and when in a redox reaction, it

SUPPLEMENT forms Mn^{2+} ions.

a What colour is potassium manganate(VII)?

.... [1]

b What colour are the Mn^{2+} ions?

.... [1]

c What has happened to the potassium manganate(VII) in this reaction?

.... [1]

The characteristic properties of acids and bases

Student's Book pages 182–187 | Syllabus learning objectives 7.1.1–7.1.8;
SUPPLEMENT 7.1.9–7.1.12

....

1 Complete the following table.

Solution	Colour of litmus	Colour of methyl orange
Sodium hydroxide		
Sulfuric acid		

[4]

2 Complete the following table about the use of universal indicator paper.

> **TIP**
>
> You need to be very familiar with the pH scale.

Type of solution	pH value
Neutral	
Strongly acidic	
Weakly alkaline	
Weakly acidic	

[4]

3 Acids react with metals such as magnesium. Write a balanced equation, including state symbols, for the reaction between magnesium and dilute hydrochloric acid.

.... [2]

4 Nitric acid reacts with carbonates such as calcium carbonate.

a Write a word equation for this reaction.

.... [1]

b Write a balanced equation, including state symbols, for the reaction.

.... [2]

TIP
You need to ensure you can write balanced equations for the reactions you need to understand.

5 What name is given to the reaction which takes place between an acid and an alkali and produces water?

.... [1]

6 Complete the following table.

Type of aqueous solution	Ions present
Acid	
Alkali	

[2]

7 Give a definition of the term alkali.

PPLEMENT

.... [1]

TIP
At Supplementary level, this is more than the effect on indicators.

8 Look at the equation below:

PPLEMENT

$$CH_3COOH\ (aq) \rightleftharpoons CH_3COO\text{-}(aq)\ +\ H^+(aq)$$

a What is the name of the acid with the formula CH_3COOH?

.... [1]

b The acid is a weak acid. Explain what a weak acid is.

....

.... [2]

c How is a strong acid different from a weak acid?

....

.... [2]

d Give an example of a strong acid.

.... [1]

Oxides

Student's Book pages 187–189 | Syllabus learning objectives 7.2.1;
SUPPLEMENT 7.2.2–7.2.3

1 Which of the following is **not** a basic oxide?

A Zinc oxide

B Aluminium oxide

C Sodium oxide

D Sulfur dioxide

[1]

2 Zinc oxide is an amphoteric oxide. Explain what is meant by the term amphoteric.

PPLEMENT

....

.... [2]

3 Carbon dioxide reacts with water to form carbonic acid (H_2CO_3).

PPLEMENT

Write a symbol equation for this reaction.

.... [2]

Preparation of salts

Student's Book pages 189–195 | Syllabus learning objectives 7.3.1–7.3.3;
SUPPLEMENT 7.3.4–7.3.5

1

a Explain the meaning of the term soluble.

.... [1]

b Explain the meaning of the term insoluble.

.... [1]

2 Some salts are hydrated. What does this term mean?

.... [1]

3 Which of the following salts (**A**–**D**) is soluble in water?

A Calcium carbonate

B Copper(II) nitrate

C Barium sulfate

D Lead(II) hydroxide

[1]

4 Zinc sulfate crystals can be prepared using the reaction between solid zinc carbonate and dilute sulfuric acid.

a Write a word equation for this reaction. [1]

....

b Write a fully balanced equation for this reaction. [2]

....

TIP
In the preparation of a soluble salt, there are many different stages, each using different apparatus.

c Describe a method for preparing zinc sulfate crystals, a soluble salt, in the laboratory. In your method, be organised in stages. You should include:

i Which of the two reactants should be in excess.

ii The apparatus needed at each stage in the preparation and what happens at each stage of the preparation.

....

....

....

....

....

.... [4]

5 Copper(II) carbonate can be prepared using copper(II) nitrate solution and sodium
carbonate solution. The three stages of the preparation are summarised below:
PPLEMENT

Stage 1. 30 cm^3 of copper(II) nitrate solution is mixed with 30 cm^3 of sodium carbonate solution. The copper(II) carbonate forms as a precipitate.

Stage 2. The copper(II) carbonate is separated from the solutions.

Stage 3. The solid copper(II) carbonate is dried.

a What apparatus is needed for Stage 1?

.... [1]

b What is a precipitate?

.... [1]

c Sketch and label the apparatus you would use for Stage 2.

[2]

d Write a symbol equation for the reaction.

.... [2]

6 A student has written 'hydrated copper(II) sulfate is a mixture'. Is this statement true or
false? Explain your answer.
UPPLEMENT

....

.... [2]

Arrangement of elements

Student's Book pages 210–214 | Syllabus learning objectives 8.1.1–8.1.5;
SUPPLEMENT 8.1.6

1 Below is a representation of the Periodic Table with some of the elements marked with letters.

																	e
	a																
							c									d	
	b																

TIP

You do not need to learn the arrangement of the elements in the Periodic Table – a Periodic Table will be provided in your exams.

---

a Which element is in Group VII?

.... [1]

b Which elements are in the same group?

.... [1]

c Which elements are in the same period?

.... [1]

d Which elements are non-metals?

.... [1]

e Which elements will form positive ions?

.... [1]

f Which element has a full outer shell of electrons?

.... [1]

g Which element will form an ion with a charge of −1?

.... [1]

h Which element will have the greatest proton number/atomic number?

.... [1]

i Which elements will have very similar chemical properties?

.... [1]

j Element *a* reacts with water to form hydrogen. Which element will have a similar reaction with water?

.... [1]

2 What ions would you expect the following elements to form?

a Lithium

.... [1]

b Fluorine

.... [1]

c Nitrogen

.... [1]

3 Explain why lithium, sodium and potassium have very similar chemical properties.

....

.... [2]

4 The following table shows some physical properties for the first three elements in
SUPPLEMENT Group I of the Periodic Table.

TIP

It may help you to know the
density of iron is 7.86 g/cm^3.

Element	Melting point (°C)	Boiling point (°C)	Density g/cm^3
Lithium	180	1342	0.53
Sodium	98	883	0.97
Potassium	64	759	0.86

What trends can you identify in the melting point, boiling point and density information from
the table?

....

....

.... [3]

Group I properties

Student's Book pages 218–222 | Syllabus learning objectives 8.2.1–8.2.2

1   Which of the following statements about sodium is **untrue**?

    A   Sodium reacts with water to form sodium hydroxide, an alkali.

    B   Sodium is stored under oil.

    C   Sodium is a soft metal which is easily cut.

    D   Sodium has the highest melting point of the elements in Group I.

[1]

2   Which of the following statements is correct?

    A   The Group I elements are unreactive metals.

    B   Potassium is the most reactive of the metals in the group.

    C   Potassium has a higher density than lithium.

    D   The Group I elements have high melting points.

[1]

> **TIP**
>
> You may need to revise atomic structure from an earlier topic.

3   Potassium has a proton number/atomic number of 19.

a   What is the electron arrangement in potassium?

[1]

b   What ion does potassium form in its compounds?

.... [1]

c   Explain why all the elements in Group I form ions with the same charge.

....

.... [2]

4   Potassium reacts with oxygen to form potassium oxide. Write a balanced equation for this reaction.

.... [2]

5   Sodium oxide reacts with water to form sodium hydroxide.

a   Is sodium oxide an acidic or basic oxide?

.... [1]

b   Predict the pH of a solution of sodium hydroxide.

.... [1]

c   Write a balanced equation for the reaction of sodium oxide with water.

.... [2]

6   Sodium is added to some distilled water in a large beaker. State **two** observations you would expect to see.

....

.... [2]

Group VII properties

Student's Book pages 225–233 | Syllabus learning objectives 8.3.1–8.3.4

....

1 ▷ Explain the meaning of the term diatomic.

.... [1]

2 ▷ Fluorine is in Group VII.

a Use your knowledge about chlorine, bromine and iodine to predict whether fluorine is a solid, liquid or gas.

.... [1]

b How would you expect the reactivity of fluorine to compare to that of chlorine?

.... [1]

c When fluorine forms compounds, what ion does it form?

.... [1]

d Use your knowledge of atomic structure to explain why an element in Group VII will form this ion.

....

.... [2]

3 ▷ When chlorine is bubbled into a solution of sodium bromide, an orange/brown solution is formed. This is an example of a displacement reaction.

a What substance is responsible for the formation of the orange/brown solution?

.... [1]

71

b State what a displacement reaction is.

....

.... [2]

c Write a word equation for the reaction between chlorine gas and sodium bromide solution.

.... [1]

d Write a balanced equation for the reaction between chlorine gas and sodium bromide solution.

.... [2]

TIP
At Supplementary level, you will need to write ionic equations. If revision is needed, revisit the section on Stoichiometry in the Student's Book.

4 The reaction described in Question 3 is a redox reaction.

SUPPLEMENT

a What is a redox reaction?

.... [1]

b Complete and balance the following ionic equation for the reaction described in Question 3.

$Cl_2(g) + Br^-(aq) \rightleftharpoons$ .... + ... [2]

Transition elements; Noble gases

Student's Book pages 234–236 | Syllabus learning objectives 8.4.1; SUPPLEMENT 8.4.2 ; 8.5.1

....

1 Which of the following is **not** a typical characteristic of transition elements?

   A They form compounds with colours such as blue, green or brown.

   B They react vigorously when in contact with water.

   C They act as catalysts in industrial processes.

   D They are often used in construction.

.... [1]

2 Copper is a transition metal whereas sodium is an alkali metal. Describe **three** differences in physical properties between these metals.

....

....

....

.... [3]

3 Helium is a monatomic gas. Explain what this means.

.... [1]

TIP
In your exams, you will have a Periodic Table (included on page 124) to use when answering these questions.

4 Neon is a very unreactive element.

a What is proton number/atomic number of neon?

.... [1]

b How are the electrons arranged in an atom of neon?

.... [1]

c Use the electronic configuration to explain why neon is so unreactive.

....

.... [2]

5 Iron forms compounds such as iron(II) chloride and iron(III) chloride.

SUPPLEMENT

a What do the (II) and (III) symbols tell you about the iron in these compounds?

....

.... [2]

b In the presence of chlorine gas, iron(II) chloride solution can be converted into iron(III) chloride solution.

i Does this change mean that the iron has been oxidised or reduced? Explain your answer.

....

.... [2]

ii Write an equation for the reaction between iron(II) chloride solution and chlorine gas.

.... [2]

iii An ionic equation for this reaction is shown below. Balance this ionic equation:

$$\_\_\_Fe^{2+}(aq) + \_\_\_Cl_2(g) \rightarrow \_\_\_Fe^{3+}(aq) + \_\_\_Cl^-(aq)$$ [2]

Properties of metals

Student's Book pages 242–244 | Syllabus learning objectives 9.1.1–9.1.2

....

1 Which of the following is **not** a common/general physical property of a metal?

    A Low melting point

    B Good conductor of electricity

    C Malleable

    D Good conductor of heat

    .... [1]

2 A student sets up some apparatus to test the electrical conductivity of an element. Draw and label the apparatus the student could have used.

[3]

3 Metals are often ductile. Explain what this term means.

.... [1]

4 For each of the following reactions (**a–c**), write a word equation and a balanced symbol equation.

a Sodium burns in air.

i Word equation:

.... [1]

ii Symbol equation:

.... [2]

b Magnesium reacting with steam.

i Word equation:

.... [1]

ii Symbol equation:

.... [2]

c Zinc reacting with dilute hydrochloric acid.

i Word equation:

.... [1]

ii Symbol equation:

.... [2]

5 ▶ Draw and label the apparatus that can be used in the reaction between magnesium and dilute sulfuric acid to collect the gas produced.

[3]

Uses of metals; Alloys and their properties

Student's Book pages 244–246 | Syllabus learning objectives 9.2.1; 9.3.1–9.3.4;
SUPPLEMENT 9.3.5

1 ▶ Aluminium is used in the manufacture of aircraft, usually in the form of an alloy.

a Define the term alloy.

.... [1]

b Give a reason why aluminium is used in the manufacture of aircraft.

.... [1]

c Why is the aluminium used in aircraft manufacture in the form of an alloy?

.... [1]

TIP
Aluminium is widely used in many industries. Later in the Metals section, you will look at the process of extracting aluminium from its ore – it is too reactive a metal to exist in the ground as an element.

2 Give **two** reasons why copper is used in electrical wiring.

....

.... [2]

3 Which **one** of the following statements (**A–D**) best explains the use of aluminium in metal cans for storing food?

A Aluminium has a high melting point.

B Aluminium resists oxidation and corrosion generally.

C Aluminium has low density.

D Aluminium conducts electricity.

.... [1]

4 Give **two** reasons why stainless steel is often used to make kitchen knives.

....

.... [2]

5 Is an alloy a compound or a mixture? Explain your answer.

....

.... [2]

6 **a** Sketch diagrams to show the difference in the arrangement of the atoms in aluminium and in an alloy of aluminium.

[2]

b Use the diagrams to explain why an aluminium alloy is stronger than the pure metal.

....

....

....

....

[2]

• •

Reactivity series

Student's Book pages 247–251 | Syllabus learning objectives 9.4.1–9.4.3;
SUPPLEMENT 9.4.4–9.4.5

....

1 The reactivity series of metals often includes the non-metal hydrogen. Suggest a reason for this.

....

....

[2]

2 Sodium is more reactive than silver. Explain this in terms of the electron configurations of the two metals.

....

....

[1]

3 ▶ The following table shows the results of a series of experiments performed with elements listed in the reactivity series.

Element	Reaction with cold water?	Reaction with steam?	Reaction with dilute hydrochloric acid?
W	No	No	No
Y	Yes	Yes	Yes
Z	No	Yes	Yes

a   Arrange the elements (W–Z) in order of reactivity starting with the most reactive.

.... [1]

b   Complete the following table by suggesting a possible name for each of the elements.   [3]

Element	Possible name
W	
Y	
Z	

4 ▶

a   Name a metal which, when added to cold water, floats on the surface and catches fire.

.... [1]

b   Write a word equation for the reaction between this metal and water.

.... [1]

c   Write a balanced equation for the reaction between this metal and water.

.... [2]

5 The reactivity series is made up mostly of metals. Explain why it is common to include carbon in the reactivity series.

....

....

[1]

> **TIP**
>
> You need to be familiar with ionic half-equations. Visit the Electrolysis section if you need to revise how to write these equations.

6

SUPPLEMENT

a Potassium is above iron in the reactivity series. What does this tell you about the tendency of the two elements to form positive ions?

.... [1]

b What ion does potassium form? Explain how you know this.

....

.... [2]

c Write an ionic equation showing the formation of a potassium ion from a potassium atom.

.... [1]

7 Look at the following equation:

SUPPLEMENT

$$Mg(s) + CuSO_4(aq) \rightarrow MgSO_4(aq) + Cu(s)$$

a What name is given to reactions of this sort?

.... [1]

b What does the equation tell you about the relative reactivities of magnesium and copper?

.... [1]

c Rewrite the equation as an ionic equation showing only the magnesium and copper (not the sulfate).

.... [2]

d Name another metal, other than magnesium, which will undergo a similar reaction with the copper(II) sulfate solution.

.... [1]

8

SUPPLEMENT

The reactivity series shows aluminium as a reactive metal between magnesium and zinc. Why is aluminium so resistant to hot water and often used to make pans for cooking?

.... [1]

• •

Corrosion of metals

Student's Book pages 251–252 | Syllabus learning objectives 9.5.1–9.5.3; SUPPLEMENT 9.5.4–9.5.5

....

1 Rust is hydrated iron(III) oxide.

a What does the term hydrated mean?

.... [1]

b What is the chemical formula for iron(III) oxide?

.... [1]

c **i** When iron rusts to form iron(III) oxide, is this process oxidation or reduction?

.... [1]

ii Explain your answer.

.... [1]

2 Which of the following methods will **not** prevent the rusting of iron?

A Coating the iron with plastic.

B Adding carbon to the iron.

C Painting the iron.

D Greasing the iron.

.... [1]

3 What are barrier methods and how do they prevent rusting?

....

.... [2]

TIP
You may need to revise oxidation and reduction in terms of electron transfer – covered in the Redox topic.

4 The rusting of iron can be prevented by galvanising.

PPLEMENT

a Explain what galvanising is.

.... [1]

b Galvanising is a process known as sacrificial protection.

i Is iron or zinc higher in the reactivity series?

.... [1]

ii Which of the metals, iron or zinc, forms positive ions most readily?

.... [1]

iii When iron or zinc atoms form positive ions, is this process oxidation or reduction? Explain your answer.

....

.... [2]

iv Write an ionic half-equation showing the formation of zinc ions from zinc atoms.

.... [2]

• •

Extraction of metals

Student's Book pages 252–258 | Syllabus learning objectives 9.6.1–9.6.3;
SUPPLEMENT 9.6.4–9.6.5

....

1

a Which of the following metals is found in nature as a pure element?

A Magnesium **C** Calcium

B Zinc **D** Silver

.... [1]

b   Give a reason for your answer.

.... [1]

2   In a blast furnace:

a   Name the **three** solid substances that are added to the furnace.

1. ....

2. ....

3. .... [3]

b   **i**   Air is blasted into the furnace and reacts to form a gas. What is this gas?

.... [1]

    ii   This gas is then reduced to form another gas. What is this gas?

.... [1]

    iii   Write a word equation for the reaction of the gas you have named in part **ii** with iron(III) oxide.

.... [1]

    iv   In the word equation in part **iii**, what is the name of the process the iron(III) oxide undergoes?

.... [1]

c   One of the products of the reactions in the blast furnace is slag. Which of the solid substances added to the furnace is part of the reaction to produce the slag?

.... [1]

TIP
Check that you are confident about the process of electrolysis. If you are not, check the Electrochemistry section.

3

a   **i**   Aluminium is extracted from a mineral containing aluminium. What is the name of this mineral?

.... [1]

ii   What is the name of the chemical compound in this mineral?

.... [1]

b   The aluminium is extracted from its mineral by electrolysis. For the electrolysis process to work, why must the mineral be in a molten state?

.... [1]

4

SUPPLEMENT

Write chemical equations for the following reactions involved in the extraction of iron in the blast furnace:

a   The formation of carbon monoxide.

.... [2]

b   The reaction of carbon monoxide with iron(III) oxide.

.... [2]

c   The formation of slag.

.... [2]

5 The diagram shows apparatus used to extract aluminium from aluminium oxide.

PPLEMENT

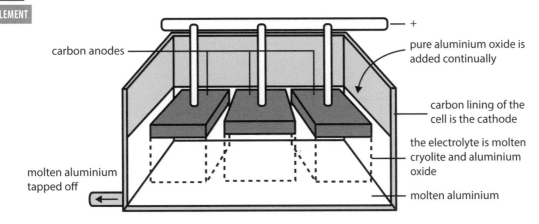

a Why is the cryolite added to the aluminium oxide?

.... [1]

b **i** At which electrode will the aluminium metal form?

.... [1]

ii Write a half-equation for the formation of the aluminium.

.... [2]

iii What will be formed at the other electrode?

.... [1]

iv Write a half-equation for the formation of this other product.

.... [2]

v Explain why the carbon anodes need to be replaced regularly.

.... [1]

Water; Fertilisers

Student's Book pages 266–271 | Syllabus learning objectives 10.1.1–10.1.7; 10.2.1–10.2.2

1 Answer these questions about natural water sources.

a Water from natural sources contains dissolved oxygen. Why is this beneficial?

[1]

b Water from natural sources can contain phosphates. Give **two** sources of these phosphates:

1. [1]

2. [1]

c Name a damaging effect these phosphates have.

[1]

d What effect does untreated sewage have on the water?

[1]

e Name a problem that is caused by having plastic pollution in the natural water supply.

[1]

2 The domestic water we use in our homes is treated in a number of stages.

a What process is used to remove solids?

[1]

b What is added to remove odours?

[1]

c Chlorine is also used. What does the chlorine do?

.... [1]

3 Describe how to test water to see if it is pure. State what result would confirm that the water is pure.

....

.... [2]

TIP
You will need to remember some of the work you have done on salts in the Student's Book – Chapter 7.

4 Anhydrous copper(II) sulfate can be used to detect the presence of water.

a What does the word anhydrous mean?

.... [1]

b If water is present, what colour change will occur when adding the liquid to the anhydrous copper(II) sulfate?

....

.... [2]

c What is the name of the substance formed if water is present?

.... [1]

5 Many common fertilisers are NPK fertilisers. What do these fertilisers contain?

.... [1]

6 Ammonium salts and nitrates are also used as fertilisers. What is the formula of ammonium nitrate?

.... [1]

Air quality and climate

Student's Book pages 271–279 | Syllabus learning objectives 10.3.1–10.3.6;
SUPPLEMENT 10.3.7–10.3.9

....

1 What is the percentage of oxygen in the air?

A 21%

B 15%

C 78%

D 10%

.... [1]

TIP
Most of the gases that are common pollutants are oxides of non-metals.

2 In which of the following situations will methane be released into the atmosphere?

A Burning petrol in a car engine.

B The incomplete burning of natural gas.

C From the digestive systems of animals like cows.

D Lightning strikes in the atmosphere.

.... [1]

3 When carbon in the form of coal is burnt:

a Which gas is formed if there is plenty of oxygen?

.... [1]

b Which gas is formed if the amount of oxygen is very small?

.... [1]

4 Most particulates originate from the exhaust fumes of cars or lorries.

a What are particulates?

.... [1]

b Name **two** problems that particulates can cause for people living near busy roads.

1. ....

2. .... [2]

5 Which of the following gases cause acid rain in the atmosphere?

A Carbon monoxide

B Nitrogen

C Sulfur dioxide

D Neon

.... [1]

> **TIP**
>
> You may have studied photosynthesis in biology.

6 Planting trees is one way of reducing the level of greenhouse gases in the atmosphere. Explain why planting trees has this effect.

....

.... [2]

7 Name **two** other ways to reduce the levels of greenhouse gases in the atmosphere.

1. .... [1]

2. .... [1]

8 Which gas – produced in the combustion of petrol in a car – can be removed by a
SUPPLEMENT catalytic converter?

    A Nitrogen

    B Carbon dioxide

    C Oxygen

    D Nitrogen monoxide

.... [1]

9 i Describe how greenhouse gases cause global warming.
SUPPLEMENT

....

.... [2]

    ii Name a common greenhouse gas.

.... [1]

10 i Write the word equation for the process of photosynthesis.
SUPPLEMENT
.... [2]

    ii Write a balanced symbol equation for photosynthesis.

.... [2]

Fuels

Student's Book pages 294–298 | Syllabus learning objectives 11.3.1–11.3.7

....

1

a What name is given to a compound containing carbon and hydrogen only?

.... [1]

> | **TIP** |
> | You may need to check the section on Atoms, elements and compounds in the Student's Book. |

b **i** Will a compound containing carbon and hydrogen only be ionically or covalently bonded?

.... [1]

ii Explain your answer to part **i**.

.... [1]

2 The following diagram shows how crude oil is separated in industry.

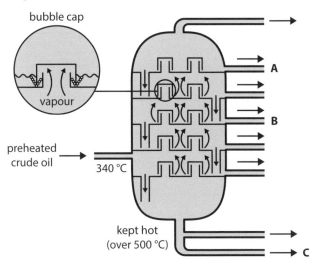

a State the name of the process for separating crude oil into its useful components.

.... [1]

b Three of the components produced in this process are petrol, kerosene and bitumen. Match the names of these three components to the letters A, B and C.

A ....

B ....

C .... [3]

c The following table shows some of the properties of the components formed in this process. Complete the table by placing ticks (✓) in the boxes to show which component has the higher value for that property.

Component	Chain length/ number of carbon atoms per molecule	Volatility/ease of forming a vapour	Boiling point	Viscosity/ thickness of the liquid
Petrol				
Bitumen				

[4]

d Complete the following table by giving a use for each of the three components.

Component	Use
Petrol	
Kerosene	
Bitumen	

[3]

3 Methane (CH_4) is the main component of natural gas.

TIP
Remember what you learnt in the Chemistry of the environment topic!

a What problem is caused by high levels of methane in the atmosphere?

.... [1]

b **i** Write a word equation for the combustion of methane.

.... [1]

ii Write a balanced symbol equation for the combustion of methane.

.... [2]

Alkanes

Student's Book pages 302–307 | Syllabus learning objectives 11.1.1–11.1.6;
SUPPLEMENT 11.1.7–11.1.9 ; 11.2.1–11.2.2; SUPPLEMENT 11.2.3 ; 11.4.1–11.4.2;
SUPPLEMENT 11.4.3–11.4.4

TIP
Activation energy is covered in the topic on chemical energetics.

1 Which of the following formulae belongs to a compound in the homologous series of alkanes?

A C_3H_6

B C_6H_{12}

C C_8H_{18}

D C_2H_2

.... [1]

2 Which of the following compounds is an alkane?

  A   Octene

  B   Decane

  C   Octanol

  D   Benzene

[1]

3 Butane is a saturated hydrocarbon and member of the homologous series of alkanes.

a What is the functional group in alkanes?

[1]

b What is a homologous series?

[1]

c What is a hydrocarbon?

[1]

d What does the term saturated mean?

[1]

e Butane has four carbon atoms in each molecule. What is the formula of butane?

[1]

f Draw a displayed formula of butane.

[1]

g Butane reacts with oxygen in a combustion reaction.

i Write a word equation for the combustion of butane in a plentiful supply of oxygen.

.... [1]

ii Write a balanced symbol equation for this reaction.

.... [2]

4 List **three** general characteristic properties of a homologous series.

PPLEMENT

1. ....

2. ....

3. .... [3]

TIP
The next two questions are challenge questions because they relate to alkanes with more than four carbon atoms.

5 Draw the displayed formula of an unbranched molecule of hexane.

PPLEMENT

[2]

6

PPLEMENT

a What is an isomer?

.... [1]

b   Draw displayed formulae of two isomers of pentane, C_5H_{12}.

[2]

7   Propane reacts with chlorine in substitution reactions.

SUPPLEMENT

a   State what a substitution reaction is.

....

.... [1]

b   In a substitution reaction, what provides the activation energy, E_a?

.... [1]

c   Draw the displayed formula of a molecule formed in this substitution reaction.

[2]

TIP
You are only required to draw products that have undergone monosubstitution – that is where only one atom or group of atoms has been replaced.

Alkenes

Student's Book pages 311–318 | Syllabus learning objectives 11.1.2;
SUPPLEMENT 11.1.7–11.1.8 ; 11.2.1; 11.2.2; SUPPLEMENT 11.2.3 ; 11.5.1–11.5.4;
SUPPLEMENT 11.5.5–11.5.6

....

1 Which of the following compounds is an alkene?

A Pentane

B A molecule with a general formula of C_nH_{2n+2}

C A molecule with a general formula of C_nH_n

D Octene

[1]

2 Is ethene a saturated or unsaturated hydrocarbon? Explain your answer.

[2]

> **TIP**
>
> You may need to refresh your memory about dot-and-cross diagrams – see the topic on Molecules and covalent bonds in the Student's Book.

3 Draw a displayed formula and a dot-and-cross diagram to show the bonding in propene.

[4]

4 ▶ The fractional distillation of crude oil produces a very low proportion of alkenes.

> **TIP**
>
> Fractional distillation was covered in the topic on alkanes.

a What is the name of the process that follows fractional distillation and which produces alkenes from alkanes?

.... [1]

b State **two** reaction conditions needed in this process:

1. .... [1]

2. .... [1]

c A test can be used to prove that alkenes have been made in this process.

i What chemical would you use in the test?

.... [1]

ii What observation would confirm the presence of an alkene?

.... [1]

5 ▶ Alkenes undergo addition reactions.

SUPPLEMENT

a What is an addition reaction?

.... [1]

b Ethene will undergo an addition reaction with hydrogen.

i What conditions are needed for this reaction?

.... [1]

ii Write an equation for this reaction.

.... [1]

iii Draw a displayed formula for the reactants and the product formed.

[2]

6 Butene forms two unbranched structural isomers.

UPPLEMENT

a Define the term structural isomer.

....

.... [1]

b Draw displayed formulae for these two unbranched isomers.

[2]

c Name the two isomers you have drawn.

....

.... [2]

Alcohols

Student's Book pages 322–328 | Syllabus learning objectives 11.1.2;
SUPPLEMENT 11.1.7 ; 11.2.1–11.2.2; SUPPLEMENT 11.2.3 ; 11.6.1–11.6.3; SUPPLEMENT 11.6.4

···

1 Which one of the compounds below belongs to the alcohol homologous series?

A C_6H_6OH

B $C_6H_{13}OH$

C C_6H_{14}

D C_6H_{12}

[1]

2 Ethanol burns in oxygen.

a Name the products of the combustion of ethanol:

i in a limited supply of oxygen.

[2]

ii in a plentiful supply of oxygen.

[2]

b Write an equation showing the combustion of ethanol in a plentiful supply of oxygen.

[2]

3 State **one** of the uses of ethanol.

[1]

4 Complete the following table which shows how ethanol is manufactured. [6]

TIP
You need to know the three important reaction conditions for the two manufacturing processes.

Method	Type of reaction	Starting material(s)	Reaction conditions
A			i Yeast ii 25–35 °C iii Absence of oxygen
B		Ethene and steam	i ii iii

5 For methods A–B in Question 4, complete the following table.

SUPPLEMENT

Method	Advantage	Disadvantage
A		
B		

[4]

6 Propan-1-ol and propan-2-ol are two unbranched alcohols.

SUPPLEMENT

a What name is given to compounds like these (i.e. they have the same molecular formulae but different structural formulae)?

.... [1]

b Draw the displayed formulae of these two unbranched alcohols.

Propan-1-ol   Propan-2-ol   [2]

· ·

Carboxylic acids

Student's Book pages 332–334 | Syllabus learning objectives SUPPLEMENT 11.1.7;
11.2.4 ; 11.7.1; SUPPLEMENT 11.7.2–11.7.3

···

1 A carboxylic acid has the structural formula: C_2H_5COOH. What is the correct name for this compound?

A Methanoic acid

B Ethanoic acid

C Propanoic acid

D Butanoic acid

[1]

2 Magnesium reacts with ethanoic acid.

a Describe what you would observe in this reaction.

[2]

b Name the **two** products formed in the reaction.

....

.... [2]

TIP
Remember: an acid has a replaceable hydrogen. Check you know which is the replaceable hydrogen in ethanoic acid.

c Write a balanced chemical equation for the reaction between ethanoic acid and magnesium.

.... [2]

TIP
You may need to refer to the topic on Acids, bases and salts for the next question.

3 Ethanoic acid reacts with bases to form a salt and water.

a What is a base?

.... [1]

b Name a base that reacts with ethanoic acid.

.... [1]

c Write a balanced equation for the reaction between ethanoic acid and the base you have named.

.... [2]

d What is the name of the salt formed in this reaction?

.... [1]

4 Ethanoic acid can be made from ethanol.

SUPPLEMENT

a What is the name of this type of reaction?

.... [1]

b Acidified aqueous potassium manganate(VII) can be used to convert ethanol into ethanoic acid. What happens to the potassium manganate(VII) in this reaction?

.... [1]

c Ethanol can also be converted to ethanoic acid during the fermentation process. Why do you think this could be a problem for a wine manufacturer?

.... [2]

5

SUPPLEMENT

a Complete the word equation:

_____ + carboxylic acid → ester + _____ [2]

b What type of catalyst is used in this reaction?

.... [1]

c If the acid is ethanoic acid and it reacts with ethanol, what would be the name of the ester formed?

.... [1]

Polymers

Student's Book pages 337–344 | Syllabus learning objectives 11.8.1–11.8.5;
SUPPLEMENT 11.8.6–11.8.13

1 Define the term monomer.

.... [1]

2 Look at the following diagram.

a What is the name of the molecules that are the reactants in the equation?

.... [1]

b What is the name of the product?

.... [1]

c What type of polymerisation is shown in the equation?

.... [1]

d State a use of the polymer produced in this reaction.

.... [1]

3

a State **two** ways that plastics can be disposed of:

1. .... [1]

2. .... [1]

TIP
There are obvious links here to the topic on Chemistry of the environment.

b For each of these ways in part **a**, describe the environmental problems they cause.

1. .... [1]

2. .... [1]

c What are the properties of many plastics that make their disposal difficult?

....

.... [2]

d Suggest ways in which the environmental effects of using plastics could be reduced.

....

....

.... [2]

4 Look at the following diagram.

SUPPLEMENT

a How many different monomers are shown in the diagram?

.... [1]

b What type of polymer is represented by the diagram?

.... [1]

c State the name of the polymer.

.... [1]

d Another polymer is called PET. What advantages does PET have compared to the polymer referred to in parts **a**, **b** and **c**?

....

.... [2]

5

PPLEMENT

```
   H      R        O
    \     |       //
     N  — C  —  C
    /     |       \
   H      H        O — H
```

a What type of compound is represented by the displayed formula shown?

.... [1]

TIP
In the molecule, there are two functional groups: an amine group and a carboxylic acid group – this might help in naming the compound.

b **i** What type of natural polymer is formed when molecules like the one shown above join together?

.... [1]

ii Draw the natural polymer formed when monomers like the one in part **a** join together.

[3]

Experimental design

Student's Book pages 356–357 | Syllabus learning objectives 12.1.1–12.1.3

1 ▸ The following diagram involves the filtration of a mixture.

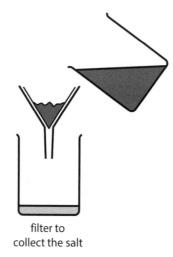

filter to
collect the salt

On the diagram, label the:

a ▸ Residue [1]

b ▸ Filtrate [1]

2 ▸ During the preparation of a salt, a solution of the salt is evaporated until crystals form when a few drops of the solution are cooled.

a ▸ State how a solution is formed.

.... [2]

b ▸ What name is given to a hot solution that forms crystals when cooled?

.... [1]

TIP
You will be familiar with the next experiment if you have completed the Rate of reaction topic.

3 The following diagram shows how the rate of reaction between solid calcium carbonate solid and hydrochloric acid varies with the concentration of the hydrochloric acid used.

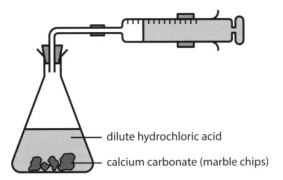

dilute hydrochloric acid

calcium carbonate (marble chips)

Four experiments are performed using the quantities shown in the following table.

Experiment	Mass of calcium carbonate (g)	Volume of 2 M hydrochloric acid (cm³)	Volume of distilled water (cm³)	Volume of gas produced in 30 seconds (cm³)
1	2	20	30	30
2	2	25	25	36
3	2	30	20	44
4	2	40	10	60

a What apparatus is used to collect the gas?

.... [1]

b What would you use to measure the mass of calcium carbonate used?

.... [1]

c What apparatus would you use to measure the time?

.... [1]

d **i** Which of the following apparatus would you use to measure the volumes of hydrochloric acid and distilled water accurately?

burette, volumetric pipette, measuring cylinder

.... [1]

ii   Explain your answer.

....   [1]

e   To ensure a fair test, a student decides to measure the temperature of the hydrochloric acid solution before it is used. What apparatus should be used?

....   [1]

• •

Acid–base titrations

Student's Book page 191 | Syllabus learning objectives 12.2.1–12.2.2

....

TIP
This experiment is a method to accurately make a salt. This is also part of the topic on Acids, bases and salts.

1   You have been asked to carry out a titration between sodium hydroxide solution and dilute hydrochloric acid to help you calculate the concentration of the dilute hydrochloric acid. This is your method:

i   Measure out 25 cm^3 of sodium hydroxide solution and put into conical flask.

ii   Measure out 50 cm^3 of dilute hydrochloric acid.

TIP
Methyl orange is a very common indicator used in acid/alkali titrations – it changes colour at the end point on the addition of 1–2 drops of the acid.

iii   Add three drops of methyl orange to the conical flask containing the sodium hydroxide solution.

iv Add the dilute hydrochloric acid slowly to the conical flask until the methyl orange changes colour. This is the trial titration. Then repeat the procedure until your results are very close.

v The results of the titration are shown in **Table 1**.

Titration	Initial volume of the acid (cm^3)	Final volume of the acid (cm^3)	Volume of the acid added (cm^3)
Trial	0.0	22.4	22.4
1st accurate	22.4	43.0	
2nd accurate	0.0		20.7

Table 1

a What apparatus would you use to measure the 25 cm^3 of sodium hydroxide solution?

.... [1]

b What apparatus would you use to measure the amount of hydrochloric acid added?

.... [1]

c Explain why the trial titration is nearly always less accurate than the titrations which follow this one.

....

.... [2]

d State the colour change in the methyl orange at the end-point of the titration.

.... [1]

e Now, complete **Table 1**. [2]

f To work out the concentration of dilute hydrochloric acid, what volume of hydrochloric acid would you use? Explain why you chose this volume.

....

.... [2]

g **i** Write a word equation, including state symbols, for the reaction in this titration experiment.

.... [2]

ii Write a symbol equation for the reaction between sodium hydroxide and hydrochloric acid.

.... [1]

TIP
Using titration results to calculate the concentration of a solution is covered in Stoichiometry.

h The concentration of the sodium hydroxide used in the titration was 0.1 M. Use the

SUPPLEMENT results of the titration to work out the concentration of the hydrochloric acid.

....

....

....

.... [3]

Chromatography

Student's Book pages 357–361 | Syllabus learning objectives 12.3.1–12.3.2;
SUPPLEMENT 12.3.3–12.3.4

1 Paper chromatography has been used to find out how many dyes there are in a sample of black ink. The apparatus and the chromatogram formed in the experiment are also shown below.

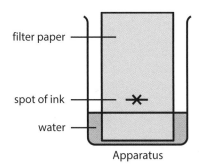

Apparatus

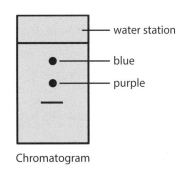

Chromatogram

a Why is the water level in the beaker below the spot of ink?

.... [1]

b No ink is left on the cross after 20 minutes when the water has soaked up to almost the top of the filter paper. Explain what this tells you about the black ink.

.... [1]

c Is the black ink a mixture or a pure substance? Explain your answer.

....

.... [1]

2 Paper chromatography is used to identify the components of a dye labelled M on the following chromatogram.

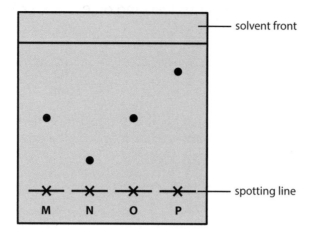

Which of the following statements is correct?

A The dye M contains substances N, O and P.

B The dye M contains substances O and P.

C The dye M contains substance O.

D The dye O is the most soluble substance in the solvent used.

.... [1]

TIP
In your experiments, you will probably have used coloured substances. In analytical laboratories, paper chromatography can also be used for colourless substances.

3

SUPPLEMENT

The components of colourless substances can be separated by chromatography. How can the components be identified?

.... [1]

a The R_f value of a component can be used to identify a substance. State the formula used to calculate an R_f value.

.... [1]

b Study the following chromatogram.

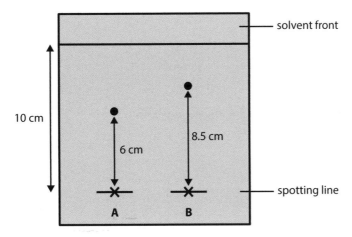

i What is the R_f value of substance A?

....

.... [1]

ii What is the R_f value of substance B?

....

.... [1]

Separation and purification

Student's Book pages 360–364 | Syllabus learning objectives 12.4.1–12.4.3

1 For each of the following mixtures (**a**–**d**), state the method of separation that could be used.

a Salt solution and sand.

.... [1]

b Common salt and lumps of marble (calcium carbonate).

.... [1]

c Sodium chloride from a saturated solution of sodium chloride.

.... [1]

d Water from a solution of sodium chloride.

.... [1]

2 A hot solution of sodium chloride solution is left to crystallise. What processes are needed for crystals of sodium chloride to form?

....

.... [2]

3 Why is fractional distillation used in some separations rather than simple distillation?

....

.... [2]

4 Look at the following apparatus.

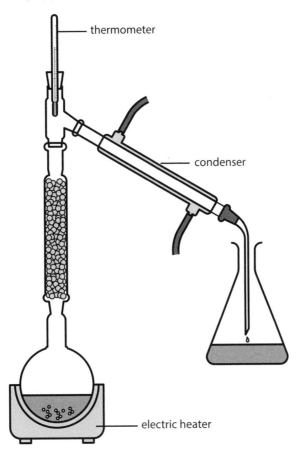

thermometer

condenser

electric heater

a What is the name of the process this apparatus is used for?

.... [1]

b Name **two** substances that could be separated using this apparatus:

1. .... [1]

2. .... [1]

c Explain why this method separates these two substances.

.... [1]

d   How could you check to see if the liquid collected in the conical flask is a pure substance?

....

....   [2]

e   Which industrial process uses this method?

....   [1]

> **TIP**
>
> You will have covered this process in your study of fuels.

5   What method could be used to find out if a sample of a solid was pure? Explain your answer.

....

....   [2]

Identification of ions and gases

Student's Book pages 368–375 | Syllabus learning objectives 12.5.1–12.5.4

1   Which of the following solutions contains Br^- ions?

A   It forms a white precipitate with dilute nitric acid and silver nitrate.

B   It forms a white precipitate with dilute nitric acid and barium nitrate.

C   Red litmus turns blue with warm sodium hydroxide solution and aluminium.

D   It forms a cream precipitate with dilute nitric acid and silver nitrate.

.... Identification of ions and gases ....   [1]

2 Which of the following is a test for hydrogen gas?

    A   It relights a glowing splint.

    B   It produces a popping sound with a lighted splint.

    C   It turns damp litmus paper blue.

    D   It turns limewater cloudy.

.... [1]

3

a Describe how to perform a flame test.

....

....

.... [3]

b What colour flame would be produced on testing sodium chloride?

.... [1]

4 Some dilute sodium hydroxide is added to a solution of copper(II) sulfate.

a What would you expect to observe?

.... [1]

b What would you observe if dilute ammonia solution was added to copper(II) sulfate followed by excess dilute ammonia solution?

....

.... [2]

TIP
A cation is a positive ion which would be attracted to the cathode in electrolysis.

5 ▶ Complete the following table which shows the results of adding a test chemical/reagent to a solution containing a cation.

Cation	Test chemical	Result
Fe^{2+}		Green precipitate forms
	Sodium hydroxide solution added	Reddish-brown precipitate forms
Zn^{2+} or Al^{3+}		White precipitate forms but dissolves when excess chemical is added
NH_4^+		Damp red litmus turns blue

[4]

6 ▶ You are provided with a white powder sample which you think may be calcium carbonate. Complete the following table with the results that would confirm that the powder *is* calcium carbonate.

Ion	Test	Result
Ca^{2+}		
CO_3^{2-}		

[4]

7 The results of two tests on a white powder are shown in the following table.

Test	Result
Flame test	A light purple flame is produced
Add a mixture of nitric acid and barium nitrate	A white precipitate is formed

Suggest the name of the white powder.

....

.... [2]

TIP
Ionic equations are covered in Stoichiometry in the Student's Book.

8 Write an ionic equation for each of the reactions **a–c**.

PLEMENT

a Chromium ions reacting with hydroxide ions.

.... [1]

b Sulfate ions reacting with barium ions.

.... [1]

c Ammonium ions reacting with hydroxide ions.

.... [1]

The Periodic Table of elements

The Periodic Table of Elements

Key

atomic number
atomic symbol
name
relative atomic mass

Group

I	II											III	IV	V	VI	VII	VIII
																	2 **He** helium 4
3 **Li** lithium 7	4 **Be** beryllium 9											5 **B** boron 11	6 **C** carbon 12	7 **N** nitrogen 14	8 **O** oxygen 16	9 **F** fluorine 19	10 **Ne** neon 20
11 **Na** sodium 23	12 **Mg** magnesium 24							1 **H** hydrogen 1				13 **Al** aluminium 27	14 **Si** silicon 28	15 **P** phosphorus 31	16 **S** sulfur 32	17 **Cl** chlorine 35.5	18 **Ar** argon 40
19 **K** potassium 39	20 **Ca** calcium 40	21 **Sc** scandium 45	22 **Ti** titanium 48	23 **V** vanadium 51	24 **Cr** chromium 52	25 **Mn** manganese 55	26 **Fe** iron 56	27 **Co** cobalt 59	28 **Ni** nickel 59	29 **Cu** copper 64	30 **Zn** zinc 65	31 **Ga** gallium 70	32 **Ge** germanium 73	33 **As** arsenic 75	34 **Se** selenium 79	35 **Br** bromine 80	36 **Kr** krypto 84
37 **Rb** rubidium 85	38 **Sr** strontium 88	39 **Y** yttrium 89	40 **Zr** zirconium 91	41 **Nb** niobium 93	42 **Mo** molybdenum 96	43 **Tc** technetium –	44 **Ru** ruthenium 101	45 **Rh** rhodium 103	46 **Pd** palladium 106	47 **Ag** silver 108	48 **Cd** cadmium 112	49 **In** indium 115	50 **Sn** tin 119	51 **Sb** antimony 122	52 **Te** tellurium 128	53 **I** iodine 127	54 **Xe** xenon 131
55 **Cs** caesium 133	56 **Ba** barium 137	57–71 lanthanoids	72 **Hf** hafnium 178	73 **Ta** tantalum 181	74 **W** tungsten 184	75 **Re** rhenium 186	76 **Os** osmium 190	77 **Ir** iridium 192	78 **Pt** platinum 195	79 **Au** gold 197	80 **Hg** mercury 201	81 **Tl** thallium 204	82 **Pb** lead 207	83 **Bi** bismuth 209	84 **Po** polonium –	85 **At** astatine –	86 **Rn** radon –
87 **Fr** francium –	88 **Ra** radium –	89–103 actinoids	104 **Rf** rutherfordium –	105 **Db** dubnium –	106 **Sg** seaborgium –	107 **Bh** bohrium –	108 **Hs** hassium –	109 **Mt** meitnerium –	110 **Ds** darmstadtium –	111 **Rg** roentgenium –	112 **Cn** copernicium –	113 **Nh** nihonium –	114 **Fl** flerovium –	115 **Mc** moscovium –	116 **Lv** livermorium –	117 **Ts** tennessine –	118 **Og** oganesson –

lanthanoids

57 **La** lanthanum 139	58 **Ce** cerium 140	59 **Pr** praseodymium 141	60 **Nd** neodymium 144	61 **Pm** promethium –	62 **Sm** samarium 150	63 **Eu** europium 152	64 **Gd** gadolinium 157	65 **Tb** terbium 159	66 **Dy** dysprosium 163	67 **Ho** holmium 165	68 **Er** erbium 167	69 **Tm** thulium 169	70 **Yb** ytterbium 173	71 **Lu** lutetium 175

actinoids

89 **Ac** actinium –	90 **Th** thorium 232	91 **Pa** protactinium 231	92 **U** uranium 238	93 **Np** neptunium –	94 **Pu** plutonium –	95 **Am** americium –	96 **Cm** curium –	97 **Bk** berkelium –	98 **Cf** californium –	99 **Es** einsteinium –	100 **Fm** fermium –	101 **Md** mendelevium –	102 **No** nobelium –	103 **Lr** lawrencium –

The volume of one mole of any gas is 24 dm^3 at room temperature and pressure (r.t.p.).